THE
HOLY
SPIRIT

Jay Wilson, evangelist
1233 N. 8th
Bozeman, MT 59715
Ph: 406-581-2930, 406-586-8061
www.newcreationstudies.org
www.christschurchonline.com
email: wilsonj@mcn.net

Dear Reader,

This Bible study is the third in a series designed to teach you the basics of the New Testament. It is our prayer that it will accomplish its purpose

The basic conclusions reached in this study are as follows:

1. The Holy Spirit is adequately represented by Jesus Christ.

2. The baptism with the Holy Spirit occurred only twice—once to begin the church, and once to extend salvation to the Gentiles. It consisted of:

    a) A sound like a mighty rushing wind
    b) Tongues like fire
    c) Speaking in other languages

3. The indwelling presence of the Holy Spirit is given at an individual's immersion into Christ.

4. The gifts of the Holy Spirit were given through the laying on of the apostles' hands, and were necessary for the early church to function in the absence of the written New Testament. With the death of the apostles, the presence of the gifts of the Holy Spirit on earth gradually ceased.

5. There were some special evidences of the Holy Spirit at critical points very early in the development of the New Testament church.

We want to stress that it is important that we let God define in the New Testament what He means when He gives a name to a certain manifestation of the Spirit, and that He provides these manifestations through means very clearly—and undeviatingly—laid out in the Bible.

We want to remind the reader that the author of this booklet is an uninspired human being, subject to error and ignorance. You must go to the Bible itself for answers.

The New American Standard Version of the Bible was used in preparation of this study, and is quoted throughout.

Your servant,

Jay Wilson

"The Bible only . . . makes Christians only

THE HOLY SPIRIT

Jay Wilson

THE HOLY SPIRIT

Introduction:

- Jesus said: "And I will ask the Father, and He will give you another Helper, that He may be with you forever; that is, the Spirit of truth" (John 14:16,17).
- "When the Helper comes, He will bear witness of Me…" (John 15:26).
- "He shall glorify Me…" (John 16:14).

Outline

1. Who is the Holy Spirit?
2. The baptism with the Holy Spirit
3. The indwelling presence of the Holy Spirit
4. The gifts of the Holy Spirit
5. The filling with the Holy Spirit

I. Who Is The Holy Spirit?

A. *The Godhead, Deity*

- We immerse into the name of the Father, Son, and Holy Spirit (**Matthew 28:19,20**)

- **Genesis 1:26**—Let Us make man in Our image

- **Romans 1:20; Acts 17:29**—Divine Nature

B. *The revelation of God*

- Difficulty in understanding an infinite God

- **John 14:8–11**—Christ is the Father in the flesh

C. *Jesus is the revelation of the Holy Spirit*

- **Colossians 1:19**—It was the Father's good pleasure for all the fulness to dwell in Him

- **John 14:16**—Another Helper, who was with them already

- *Paracletos*—Person called alongside to help

- **I John 2:1**—Jesus is also the *Paracletos*

- **John 16:7**—It is to your advantage that I go away

D. *Other name for the Spirit*

- **Romans 8:9–11**—The Spirit, the Spirit of God, the Spirit of Christ, Christ in you, the Spirit of Him who raised Christ from the dead, and His Spirit who indwells you

>∼The Holy Spirit is one of the three persons of the Godhead. If you want to find out who the Holy Spirit is, find out who Jesus is. The Holy Spirit is who Jesus would be if He ministered in the spirit rather than in the flesh.∼✕

II. The Baptism With The Holy Spirit

    A. *The baptism with the Holy Spirit promised*
       Mark 1:8—John the Immerser promised that Jesus would baptize with the Holy Spirit

       Acts 1:1–11—Jesus promised the apostles that they would be baptized with the Holy Spirit within a few days

       Acts 1:12–15—Among the 120 disciples were "the women," a reference back to Mary and Martha [and others], who were Judeans (John 11:18,19)

    B. *The baptism with the Holy Spirit on the Day of Pentecost*
       Acts 2:1—The Day of Pentecost came ten days after Jesus' ascension and the place was the Temple

       Acts 2:2–4—The sound like a mighty rushing wind, the tongues like fire, and the speaking in foreign languages

       Acts 2:6—The Jews came together

       Acts 2:7—Those who were filled with the Spirit were all Galileans; the apostles were all Galileans

       Acts 2:22–36—The first gospel sermon

       Acts 2:37–42—3000 received Peter's word and were immersed; the beginning of the church

    C. *The baptism with the Spirit and the household of Cornelius*
       Salvation only for Jews and Samaritans for 10–13 years after church's beginning

       Acts 10:1–8—Preparation of Cornelius

       Acts 10:9–23—Preparation of Peter

       Acts 10:23–43—Peter meets and speaks to Cornelius' friends and relatives

       Acts 10:44–48—The gift of the Holy Spirit is poured out on Gentiles; Peter and Jewish Christians amazed; Peter commands immersion in water

Acts 11:1–3—Jewish Christians in Jerusalem take exception to Peter's going to the Gentiles

Acts 11:4–17—Peter explains

Acts 11:15—Peter says, "The Holy Spirit fell upon them just as He did upon us at the beginning."

Acts 11:16—Peter quotes Acts 1:5 about the "baptism with the Holy Spirit" as applying here and "at the beginning"

Acts 11:18—Jewish Christians glorify God for granting salvation to the Gentiles

The baptism with the Holy Spirit was an overwhelming sign from heaven consisting of three things:
    1) the sound like a mighty rushing wind
    2) tongues like fire
    3) speaking in other languages.

The sign was for the benefit of those of Jewish background both times it happened. The first time, the apostles were baptized with the Holy Spirit to begin the church. Approximately 10–13 years later the household of Cornelius was baptized with the Holy Spirit to show Jews that Gentiles could become Christians also.

The baptism with the Holy Spirit was not a substitute for, and did not set aside the necessity of being immersed in water in the name of Jesus for the forgiveness of sins.

III. The Indwelling Presence of the Holy Spirit

    A. *The Holy Spirit dwells within Christians*
        Romans 8:9–11
        I Corinthians 6:19
        II Timothy 1:14

    B. *When does the Holy Spirit enter into the Christian?*

        Acts 2:38—The gift of the Holy Spirit is received when a person repents and is immersed in the name of Jesus

        Acts 19:1–7—12 men from Ephesus who had been immersed for the forgiveness of sins (Mark 1:4) were immersed into the name of Jesus to receive the Holy Spirit

John 3:3–5—Entrance into the kingdom of God (the church—Matthew 16:28; Mark 9:1; Colossians 1:13) is secured upon being born of water and Spirit. Entrance into the body of Christ is secured upon immersion in water (I Corinthians 12:13). Since the body of Christ is also the church, a person must therefore receive the Holy Spirit at his immersion into the person of Christ.

>━The Holy Spirit—in His indwelling presence—comes to live in an individual at his immersion into Christ.━<

IV. The Gifts Of The Holy Spirit

A. *What are the gifts of the Spirit?*

   I Corinthians 12:4–11—the gifts listed

B. *How were the gifts given in the Bible?*

   Acts 8:12–19—The Holy Spirit was given through the laying on of the apostles' hands

   I Corinthians 14:26–33—The possessor of a spiritual gift was in control of his gift at all times

   II Timothy 1:6—Timothy was to rekindle the gift that was in him through the laying on of Paul's hands

   Acts 6:6–8—Stephen had gifts of the Holy Spirit after the apostles laid hands on him

   Acts 6:6; 8:6,7—Philip had gifts of the Holy Spirit after the apostles laid hands on him

   Acts 19:6—The 12 in Ephesus spoke in tongues and prophesied after Paul laid hands on them

C. *What was the duration of the gifts?*

   I Corinthians 13:8–13—The gifts lasted until the completion of the New Testament

D. *What was the purpose of the gifts?*

   I Corinthians 12:4–11—Each of the gifts listed had an important function in the congregation in the absence of the completed New Testament

>☞ The gifts of the Holy spirit were given by the laying on of the apostles' hands. They consisted of about ten different specialties, and were necessary in the early church. They lasted until the writings of the New Testament were completed. The user of spiritual gifts was in control at all times, and was exhorted to use his gift in a spirit of love. ☜

V. The Filling With The Holy Spirit

A. *The filling with the Holy Spirit occurred under the Old Covenant*

Luke 1:67—John the Immerser's father was filled with the Holy Spirit and prophesied

II Peter 1:21—The men of old spoke as they were moved by the Spirit

B. *The filling with the Holy Spirit occurred in the very early stages in the church's development*

Acts 4:8—Peter was filled with the Holy Spirit while on trial (Mark 13:11)

Acts 4:31—The disciples were filled with the Holy Spirit after Peter and John were threatened—apparently a sign from heaven at a critical stage in the church's development

>☞ The filling with the Holy Spirit—a special filling—occurred under very special conditions at critical stages in the development of the early church. ☜

THE HOLY SPIRIT

INTRODUCTION

Jesus said, "And I will ask the Father, and He will give you another Helper, that He may be with you forever, that is the Spirit of truth…" (John 14:16,17).

Jesus promised that He would send the Holy Spirit for Christians. How does the Spirit come to the individual? What does He do after He comes? Because of all the controversy concerning the Holy Spirit, we want definite Bible answers to our questions—we don't want mere speculation.

Confidence

In the few short years that I have been preaching and teaching, I have come to realize that the most important question is the question that Paul asked some men from Ephesus: "Did you receive the Holy Spirit when you believed?" (Acts 19:2). The reason why this is the most important question is also given by Paul: "But if anyone does not have the Spirit of Christ, he does not belong to Him" (Romans 8:9).

It is important that each of us have confidence in our salvation: "And now, little children, abide in Him, so that when He appears, we may have confidence, and not shrink away from Him in shame at His coming" (I John 2:28). Unless we are confident, and our confidence is based on what the Bible definitely says, we shall shrink away from Him in shame at His coming.

There is only one way to have that confidence. That way is to be able to prove, to yourself and others, what the Bible teaches about the Holy Spirit. All the pep talks and enthusiasm builders of this world will not give you the deep-down assurance that you have received the Holy Spirit. Only faith in, and obedience to, what the Bible very clearly says will provide that assurance.

The purpose of this study is to help you be able to say with the apostle Paul, "For God has not given us a spirit of being timid, but of power and love and discipline" (II Timothy 1:7).

1

The second point in this introduction concerns the whereabouts of teaching in the Bible regarding the Holy Spirit. Jesus said, "When the Helper comes…He will bear witness of Me…" (John 15:26), and "He shall glorify Me…" (John 16:14). The Holy Spirit was not coming to talk about Himself; He was coming to bear witness of Jesus, and to glorify Jesus.

So how do we find out about the Holy Spirit? In much the same way as we find out things about a mathematics teacher. His purpose is to teach arithmetic and algebra, but occasionally he will mention something about himself by way of example…that he has three children, or likes to fish. As the Holy Spirit teaches us about Jesus, we occasionally learn something about the Spirit Himself.

There is no section of scripture devoted exclusively to the Holy Spirit. What we learn about Him, we learn from a piece of information here, a scrap there, and another chunk over here. So in this study, we are going to be gathering scripture from all ends of the Bible, particularly the New Testament, in order to draw our conclusions.

OUTLINE

In this study, we will discuss these five points:

1. Who is the Holy Spirit?
2. The baptism with the Holy Spirit.
3. The indwelling presence of the Holy Spirit.
4. The gifts of the Holy Spirit.
5. Special filling with the Spirit.

I. WHO IS THE HOLY SPIRIT?

Most people have only a vague idea of who the Holy Spirit is. They usually picture Him as some inanimate force that puts a subtle pressure on people to do God's will. How does the Bible picture Him?

The Godhead, Deity

In Matthew 28:19, Jesus told the apostles to immerse disciples they had made "into the name of the Father and the Son and the Holy Spirit." Father, Son, and Holy Spirit are linked together as a unit, and Christ's followers are immersed into their common name. This unit is sometimes called the Trinity; more scripturally the Godhead or Deity.

Way back in the beginning, God said, "Let *Us* make man in *Our* image, according to Our likeness" (Genesis 1:26). What kind of God would say that man should be made in "Our" likeness?

We know that the Son was present in the beginning, and that all things were made through Him (John 1:1–3). We also know that the Spirit of God was moving over the surface of the waters in the beginning (Genesis 1:2). It was the Father speaking to the Son and Spirit who said, "Let Us make man in Our likeness."

Since God is Spirit (John 4:24), man also must be a spirit being in the likeness of God. The "Us" apparently have one likeness!

The unity of "Us" is spoken of by Paul as he preached in Athens: "Being then the offspring of God, we ought not to think that the Divine Nature is like gold or silver or stone, an image formed by the art and thought of man" (Acts 17:29). The "Us" have one Divine Nature, sometimes spoken of as the "Godhead."

The Holy Spirit is one of the "Godhead," a co–member with the Father and Son.

The Revelation of God

We have difficulty in understanding an infinite God. I remember as a child thinking about God existing forever, and that He had always existed. For some reason I visualized Him as sitting in one of my mother's tin measuring cups, and floating off into space forever. But my mind got boggled thinking about it, so I gave up.

I have a hard time identifying with a God who knows how many black and white hairs I have—and not only me, but everyone else as well! I can't identify with a God who merely speaks and light comes into existence; I have to labor so hard to make something simple.

And God understands my difficulty. So He took the form of a man, that I might identify with someone like me, who has human needs and desires. Shortly before Jesus' arrest, He was speaking with the apostles. In answer to Thomas' question about where Jesus was going, Jesus explained, "If you had known Me you would have known My Father also; and from now on you know Him and have seen Him" (John 14:7).

Philip then said, "Show us the Father and it is enough for us." Jesus said to him, "Have I been so long with you and yet you have not come to know Me, Philip? He who has seen Me has seen the Father; how do you say 'Show us the Father'?"

Jesus is the Father in the flesh! When you know Jesus, then you know the Father. The only way to know God is to know Jesus, for He said, "I am the way, and the truth, and the life; no one comes to the Father, but through me" (John 14:6).

And the only way to know Jesus is through the Bible!

Some people have trouble comprehending that Jesus is the Father, and yet is Himself. The question in their minds is this: If Jesus is the Father, then how could Jesus say, "Father forgive them, for they know not what they do"?

It is clear that Jesus ascribed all power and glory to God the Father: "If you loved Me, you would have rejoiced because I go to the Father, for the Father is greater than I" (John 14:28). This is evidently for our example, for Jesus, "although He was a Son, He learned obedience through the things He suffered" (Hebrews 5:8).

And the meaning of Isaiah 9:6 is clear to the unjaundiced eye: "For a Child will be born to us, a Son will be given to us; and the government will rest upon His shoulders; and His name will be called Wonderful Counselor, Mighty God, Eternal Father, Prince of Peace."

The child who was born is the Eternal Father!

There is no way logically to comprehend the fact that the Father and the Son are the same, but also different. So we just have to accept God's statement that this is the way it is. To refuse to accept this is a denial of the Deity of Christ, and a rejection of God's word. Jesus is the revelation of God.

4

Jesus is the Revelation of the Holy Spirit

Many religious people accept the fact that Jesus is the Father revealed—it is usually not questioned in the Christian world that the way to know the Father is to know Jesus. But who is the Holy Spirit? How do we come to know Him? Paul informs us: "For it was the Father's good pleasure for *all the fulness* to dwell in Him" (Colossians 1:19).

When Jesus was in the flesh, not only was He the revelation of the Father, but He also was the revelation of the Holy Spirit! In Him dwelt the fulness—not just of the Father—of the whole Deity, the whole Godhead.

Listen carefully to the words of Jesus in John 14:16,17: "And I will ask the Father, and He will give you another Helper, that He may be with you forever; that is, the Spirit of truth, whom the world cannot receive because it does not behold Him or know Him, but you know Him because He abides with you, and will be in you."

The apostles already knew the coming Helper, because He was living with them! The only possible explanation is that Jesus was the revelation of the Helper who would later live in them!

The word translated Helper (or Comforter, or Counselor) is the Greek word "*Paracletos*," which means "a person called alongside to help." The "*Paracletos*" is the Holy Spirit (John 14:6), and He is a person, not an "it."

But in I John 2:1, Jesus is specifically called *Paracletos*—our Advocate or Counselor with the Father. The relationship between Jesus and the Holy Spirit is so close as for them to be identical.

To summarize the discussion up to this point: the Holy Spirit is a personality—just as Jesus and the Father are personalities—and that personality is adequately represented by the person of Jesus Christ.

In John 16:7, Jesus said "It is to your advantage that I go away, for if I do not go away, the Helper will not come to you...." Why would it be to the apostles' advantage that Jesus go away?

Let's ask another question: When Jesus was here in the flesh, how many places could He be at one time? The answer is—one! When He was in Galilee, He was not in Jerusalem; when He was in Jerusalem, He was not in Galilee. When He lived in His fleshly body, He was limited by it.

But…if He were to come back in the Spirit form, how many places could He be at one time? He could be everywhere! So the apostles could split up and go their eleven separate ways, and in the Spirit, Jesus could still be with each one of them. It was to their advantage that He go away.

And it was not only to the apostles' advantage, but is to ours also, for He promised, "If anyone loves Me, he will keep My word; and My Father will love him, and We will come to him, and make Our abode with him" (John 14:23). Through the Holy Spirit, Father and Son dwell in every Christian.

Other Names for the Spirit

The extremely close relationship among the Father, Son and Holy Spirit is illustrated by the names given to the Spirit. For example, in just three verses, the Holy Spirit is called (Romans 8:9,11):

1. The Spirit
2. The Spirit of God
3. The Spirit of Christ
4. Christ in you

Conclusion—Who Is The Holy Spirit?

The Holy Spirit is one of the three persons of the Godhead. If you want to know who the Holy Spirit is, find out who Jesus is. The Holy Spirit is Jesus ministering in the Spirit, rather than being physically present to minister to our needs.

II. THE BAPTISM WITH THE HOLY SPIRIT

Many people today claim to have received what they call the "baptism of the Holy Ghost (or Holy Spirit)."

The Bible never speaks of a baptism *of* the Holy Spirit, but a baptism *with* the Holy Spirit.

Just as in the case of repentance or Christian immersion, there are many definitions of the baptism with the Holy Spirit. Some individuals believe that a person is baptized with the Holy Spirit when he "accepts Jesus into his heart;" others believe that the baptism with the Holy Spirit is a "second work of grace," coming after a person is "saved," and evidenced by "speaking in tongues."

Our question is: What is God's definition of the baptism with the Holy Spirit?

The Baptism With the Holy Spirit Promised

In Mark 1:8 (and in each of the other Gospels as well), John the Immerser is quoted, "I immersed you in water; but He (who is coming after me—Jesus) will baptize you with the Holy Spirit."

John promised that Jesus would baptize "you" with the Holy Spirit, but did not define who the "you" is. (See the special study in the back on *The Baptism With Fire*.)

In Acts 1:1–11, Jesus also promised the baptism with the Holy Spirit. In these verses, Luke (the words "first account" in Acts 1:1 refer back to Luke's gospel) records some very significant facts—facts which absolutely must be understood in order to be able to define what the baptism with the Holy Spirit is.

1. Jesus appeared to the apostles over a period of 40 days. The events in these 11 verses occur on that 40th day from Jesus' resurrection from the dead.

2. Jesus gathered the apostles together on that day. There is a big difference between *apostles* and *disciples*. Jesus had many disciples—He had thousands who had followed and learned from Him—and even after His resurrection there were hundreds of disciples who still believed in Him. But from His many disciples, Jesus chose 12 to be His apostles. The twelve consisted of those such as Peter and Andrew, and James and John.

3. It was the eleven remaining apostles that Jesus told to go into

Jerusalem and to wait for that which the Father had promised, "Which," He said, "you heard of from Me; for John baptized with water, but you shall be baptized with the Holy Spirit not many days from now."

The promise in Acts 1 was given only to the apostles—not to the 120 disciples (Acts 1:13–15).

4. Jesus promised the apostles that they would be baptized with the Holy Spirit *within several days.*

5. In Acts 1:11, the two men (apparently angels) called the eleven remaining apostles *"Men of Galilee."*

There were two major groups of Jews. The Judeans were from the area around Jerusalem, in the southern part of Palestine. The Galileans were from the area near the Sea of Galilee, some 40 miles to the north.

In Acts 1:12–15 a gathering of 120 disciples in an upper room is described. Among the 120 were the apostles of Jesus, His family, and some which Luke—in a clear reference back to his "first account," the gospel of Luke—lists as the "women." The women included Mary and Martha as well as others. What is significant about Mary and Martha is that they were from Bethany, which was about two miles from Jerusalem (John 11:18) in Judea! The 120 consisted of Judeans as well as Galileans.

In understanding the baptism with the Spirit, it is important to understand that the apostles were all Galileans.

The Baptism with the Holy Spirit on the Day of Pentecost

The baptism with the Holy Spirit and the events surrounding its occurrence are recorded in Acts 2:1–41. We particularly want to focus on the earlier verses of the chapter, Acts 2:1–15. Once again, we need to point out the significant things on the Day of Pentecost.

8

1. In Acts 2:1, we read, "And when the Day of Pentecost had come, they were all together in one place." What was the Day of Pentecost, and where is the "one place"?

   The Day of Pentecost was the Jewish feast day originally called the "Feast of Weeks" commemorating the beginning of the harvest (Exodus 23:14–17). The feast of the harvest began 50 days after the feast of Passover and hence came to be known as Pentecost. Jesus was killed during Passover week, arose from the dead on the first day of the following week, and ascended into heaven on the 40th day following His resurrection. The Day of Pentecost was, therefore, just 10 days after His gathering the apostles together and His ascension.

   On the Day of Pentecost, according to Old Testament Law, the Hebrew males were required to present themselves to the Lord—first at the Tabernacle, and later in Jerusalem at the Temple. In 30 A.D., the "one place" of Acts 2:1 is the Temple—it is not the upper room of Acts 1:13.

2. Then in Acts 2:2–4 we find that a tremendously powerful sign came from heaven. Three things occurred:

   - There was a sound like a mighty wind—*not a mighty wind*, but a sound like one.

   - There were tongues *like fire* which came down and sat on the heads of each of them.

   - They were speaking in other languages as the Spirit was giving them utterance.

3. We recall that Jesus had promised just ten days earlier that the apostles would be baptized with the Holy Spirit, "not many days from now." We conclude at this point that the baptism with the Holy Spirit consists of the three components listed in the previous paragraph and that only the apostles were baptized with the Spirit.

What is the evidence for our conclusion?

> **First, considering the evidence that the baptism with the Spirit consists of:**
> - The sound like a mighty rushing wind
> - The tongues like fire coming on the heads of each
> - Speaking in other languages

Descent of the Holy Spirit, Pentecost, 30 AD

    a) Jesus promised that the apostles would be baptized with the Holy Spirit "not many days from now." The events on the Day of Pentecost are the only ones that fit this time frame.

    b) John the Baptist had promised that Jesus would baptize with the Holy Spirit. Peter, speaking on this Day of Pentecost says that Jesus "poured forth this which you both see and hear" (Acts 2:33). The baptism with the Holy Spirit, sent from Jesus, was both visible and audible.

> **Secondly, considering the evidence that only the apostles were baptized with the Spirit on the Day of Pentecost:**

    a) It was only to the apostles that Jesus promised the baptism with the Spirit "not many days from now."

    b) All of those who spoke in other tongues were Galileans (Acts 2:7). Many of the 120 (Acts 1:14,15) disciples were Judeans (including Mary, Martha, and Lazarus, for example). Only the eleven remaining apostles were all Galileans (Acts 1:11).

    c) Those who spoke in other languages were accused by some of being drunk (Acts 2:13,15). Peter defended the eleven, NOT the 120 (Acts 2:14).

    d) As we have already shown, the events on the Day of Pentecost occurred in the Temple, not in the upper room (Acts 1:13).

Many of the 120 were women, and would not have been presenting themselves at the Temple as the men were required to do.

There are a number of groups today which believe that they have received the "baptism with the Holy Spirit." They believe that the evidence that a person is baptized with the Spirit is that he "speaks in tongues;" and they also believe that the 120 of Acts 1 were all baptized with the Spirit.

When we let God define what He means by the "baptism with the Holy Spirit," it is obvious that it includes not only "speaking in other languages," but also tongues like fire, and a sound like a mighty rushing wind. No one has been baptized with the Spirit unless all three are present.

It is also clear that only the apostles were baptized with the Spirit on the Day of Pentecost. And when we understand the purpose of the baptism with the Spirit, it will be clear why God only baptized the apostles with the Spirit.

The Baptism With The Holy Spirit—The Household of Cornelius

The baptism with the Holy Spirit is referred to only once more in the Bible. A Roman soldier named Cornelius and his family and friends were baptized with the Spirit in an unusual situation.

As we turn to Acts 10, we want to note some things:

1. It had been at least ten to thirteen years since the Day of Pentecost until the events of Acts 10 and 11 occurred.

2. During these years, salvation was only for the Jews and their half–breed relatives, the Samaritans.

3. There was no salvation for the Gentiles. Earlier, in Acts 9, the Lord had chosen an apostle to the Gentiles—Saul of Tarsus (later known as the great apostle Paul). But as yet, God had not opened the door of salvation to the Gentiles.

Let us now note the important points as God opens salvation for the Gentiles:

1. God began by choosing a good man. The man He selected

was a Roman centurion named Cornelius who had helped the Jews in many ways, who prayed to God, and who gave alms to the poor.

An angel appeared to Cornelius (Acts 10:1–18), and told him to send down the seacoast to the city of Joppa. In Joppa was Simon Peter, who would preach the gospel to them. Cornelius then dispatched soldiers to get Peter.

2. In the meantime (Acts 10:19–23), the Lord prepares Peter for the events that are shortly to follow.

Peter is up on the rooftop praying just before lunchtime, and he has a vision of a great sheet being let down from heaven. On the sheet are all sorts of unclean animals that a Jew should not eat (Jews could eat only mammals that both chewed the cud and had cloven hooves. Pigs had cloven hooves, but did not chew the cud, and were unclean—see Leviticus 11).

As Peter views the sheet being let down to him, a voice says to him, "Arise, Peter, kill and eat." But Peter says, "By no means, Lord, for I have never eaten anything unholy or unclean." And again the voice comes a second time, "What God has cleansed, no longer consider unholy."

This happened three times for Peter's benefit, then the whole thing was taken back up into heaven. As Peter was thinking about these things, the Holy Spirit spoke to him, telling him that there were certain men outside and that Peter was to go with them without doubting anything, for the Holy Spirit said, "I have sent them Myself."

So the next day Peter and six brethren went with these men to Cæsarea where Cornelius was waiting for them.

3. As Peter and the Jewish Christian brethren arrived, Cornelius met them and fell down to worship at Peter's feet. Peter stood him up and told Cornelius not to worship him, for he was just a man.

Then in Acts 10:28 Peter apologized for being there, explaining that it was not lawful for a Jew to go to the house of a Gentile or to eat with him, and yet the Lord told Peter and his brothers in Christ to come.

4. Cornelius had his family and friends assembled to hear what Peter had to say, so Peter began preaching to them. He testified that Jesus had been resurrected from the dead, and that in this way God proved Him to be the Messiah.

5. As Peter came to the close of his message, a very strange thing happened (Acts 10:44–48). While Peter was still speaking, the Holy Spirit fell upon the Gentiles who were there and the Jewish Christians were *amazed* because the gift of the Holy Spirit had been poured out upon the Gentiles also. They were hearing them speaking in tongues and glorifying God.

6. As a result of all this, Peter's reaction was that no one could forbid water for these to be immersed who had "received the Holy Spirit just as we did." And he ordered them to be immersed in the name of Jesus.

What is it that happened to these Gentiles? Something very amazing concerning the Holy Spirit occurred—that much is certain. But there is not enough information in Acts 10 to give us the complete picture. However, the story is retold in Acts 11, and there we find enough facts to help us put everything into focus.

1. In Acts 11:1–3, when Peter went back to Jerusalem, the Jewish Christians there took him to task for having gone to the house of Gentiles and having eaten with them. For almost 1500 years God had been impressing upon the minds of the Jews that they were a special people, a separate people, and that they were not to touch or eat with Gentiles—they were unclean.

This was so strongly impressed upon their minds that these early Christians did not understand that the gospel was to be

13

for all nations and for all peoples (John 11:52). So it became necessary for Peter to explain what happened at the house of Cornelius the Gentile.

2. He recounted how the angel had appeared to Cornelius, telling him to send to Joppa to find Peter, who would tell him "Words by which you will be saved." He pointed out how he (Peter) had seen the vision of the great sheet being let down. He described what then had happened in Cæsarea, how as he was preaching, the Holy Spirit "fell on them, just as He did upon us at the beginning" (Acts 11:15).

Acts 11:15 is a key verse in understanding the baptism with the Spirit. There are three main thoughts to consider:

a) Peter said that the Holy Spirit fell upon them as on "us at the beginning." When was the "beginning"? The "beginning" is the Day of Pentecost, 30 A.D. On that day the apostles were baptized with the Holy Spirit, and the church—the bride and body of Christ—had its beginning.

b) Peter also points out that something happened to "them" just as on "us at the beginning." The "us" is very clearly, from the record of Acts 1 & 2, the apostles.

c) Peter further points out that the Holy Spirit fell on the Gentiles "just" as He did on "us at the beginning." When someone uses the word "just" in this context, it means "in exactly the same way."

On the Day of Pentecost we recall that three things happened to the apostles:

- There was a sound like a mighty rushing wind, which filled the house where they were sitting.
- There were tongues like fire coming down on the heads of each of them.

14

- Each spoke in other tongues as the Spirit was giving them utterance.

When Peter says that it "fell on them just as on us at the beginning," we know that all three of the above were present, although the record in Acts 10 does not specify all the details.

3. In Acts 11:16 Peter defines what happened: "And I remembered the word of the Lord, how He used to say, 'John baptized with water, but you shall be baptized with the Holy Spirit.' " Peter in this way tells that the household of Cornelius was baptized with the Holy Spirit—and that the baptism with the Spirit once again consisted of the three parts listed above.

We now understand what Peter meant in Acts 10:47—God had baptized Cornelius and his household with the Spirit just as He had baptized "we" (the apostles on the Day of Pentecost).

Peter then explains in Acts 11:17 that "God gave to them the same gift as He gave to us, after believing in the Lord Jesus Christ. Who was I that I could stand in God's way?" Peter, as a result of this sign, understood that he couldn't stand in God's way—that God was going to make the way of salvation open to Gentiles regardless of what Peter wanted, and that he was not to call "unclean" (Gentiles) what the Lord was now calling cleansed.

As Peter made these things clear to the Jewish Christians back in Jerusalem, they also now understood, and said, as they glorified God, "Well, then, God has granted to the Gentiles also the repentance that leads to life" (Acts 11:18).

Baptism with the Spirit

—included three things:
  -sound like a mighty, rushing wind
  -tongues like fire
  -speaking in other languages
—was a sign for the benefit of Jewish people
—does not negate immersion in water for forgiveness of sins

The Purpose of the Baptism with the Holy Spirit

In understanding the baptism with the Spirit, it is important that we understand what its purpose was.

1. On the Day of Pentecost, recorded in Acts 2, we notice that the result of the Spirit being poured out on the apostles was that all the Jews in the Temple "came together" (Acts 2:6). Peter then preached the first gospel sermon, explaining for the first time the terms of pardon under the New Covenant. As a result of hearing the message proclaimed that day, 3000 were immersed in the name of Jesus for the forgiveness of their sins (Acts 2:41), and the church began with great power as Jesus had promised in Mark 9:1.

    On the Day of Pentecost, the purpose of the baptism with the Spirit was to be a tremendous sign to the Jews—first, so that they would gather to hear the good news proclaimed, and secondly, that they would believe the good news when it was announced.

2. Cornelius' household was also baptized with the Spirit as a sign for those of Jewish background. Because of Jewish prejudice against Gentiles, the sign was first to remove Peter's unwillingness to have the Gentiles immersed in water. Secondly, the sign provided evidence to Jewish Christians in other locations, such as Jerusalem (Peter's six brethren would provide important back–up testimony) that Gentiles were acceptable to God.

    In Cornelius' case, the baptism with the Spirit was not for the benefit of his household at all. It was strictly a sign for the benefit of the Jewish Christians that Gentiles could now obey the gospel.

3. Jesus had promised Peter, "I will give you the keys of the kingdom of heaven; and whatever you bind on earth shall

16

have been bound in heaven, and whatever you loose on earth shall have been loosed in heaven" (Matthew 16:19).

On the Day of Pentecost Peter used the keys of the kingdom to open the door of salvation to the Jews and Samaritans after the sign—the baptism with the Spirit—had been given from heaven! Again, Peter used the keys to open the door of salvation to the Gentiles after the sign—the baptism with the Spirit—had been given from heaven!

4. The only purpose of the baptism with the Spirit was to be a sign from heaven—first to begin the church, and then to open salvation to the Gentiles. In both cases the sign was for the benefit of Jews watching, and not for the benefit of those baptized with the Spirit.

Evidence for our above contention is this:

a) Jesus promised the apostles power *at the same time* as the Holy Spirit came upon them (Acts 1:8). There is no evidence that Cornelius or his household had any power at all following their being baptized with the Spirit.

b) It was necessary for Cornelius and his household to be immersed in water in Jesus' name (Acts 10:47,48) for the forgiveness of sins (Acts 2:38). (For a full understanding of this, see the lesson on God's Plan of Salvation and examine the next section in this lesson dealing with the indwelling presence of the Spirit.)

c) There is no evidence that Paul was ever baptized with the Spirit, but he had the power of an apostle of Jesus Christ.

d) There is no record in the scripture of any other baptism with the Spirit (some confuse the "gifts of the Spirit" with the "baptism with the Spirit"). If it were for the benefit of the receiver, we would expect the baptism with the Spirit to be continually present in the inspired recorded of the early church. If, however, it were merely a sign to begin the church and open salvation to the Gentiles, we would not expect to find it occurring again; and this is what we find.

Summary

The baptism with the Holy Spirit was an overwhelming sign from heaven consisting of three things:

- The sound like a mighty rushing wind
- The tongues like fire
- Speaking in other languages

The sign was for the benefit of the people of Jewish background both instances it occurred. The first time, the apostles were baptized with the Holy Spirit as a sign to Jews in the Temple, in order that the church might begin with great power. Roughly ten to thirteen years later, the household of Cornelius was baptized with the Spirit as a sign to Jewish Christians that Gentiles could now be saved also.

The baptism with the Spirit was not a substitute for, and did not set aside the necessity of being immersed in water in Jesus' name for the forgiveness of sins.

III. THE INDWELLING OF THE HOLY SPIRIT

We know from Romans 8:9, I Corinthians 6:19, and II Timothy 1:14, and other scriptures, that the Holy Spirit lives in Christians. Our question is: At what point does the Holy Spirit enter into the Christian?

Acts 2:38

In Acts 2, the apostle Peter blames the Jews for the death of the Messiah (Acts 2:36). In response to their question as to what they should do, Peter told them to repent and be immersed in the name of Jesus for the forgiveness of their sins, and they would receive the gift of the Holy Spirit.

From this we learn that, in connection with a person's repentance and his immersion in water for the forgiveness of sins, the gift of the Holy Spirit is given. What that gift is, we don't yet have enough information to know.

But it is certain that something connected with the Holy Spirit is given at a person's immersion in Christ's name.

The Power of the Indwelling Holy Spirit

Acts 19:1–6

In Acts 19 the apostle Paul came to the city of Ephesus. Before he came to this large city, a man named Apollos had been doing some powerful preaching about Jesus. But all Apollos knew was the baptism of John the Baptist, even though this was some 25 years after John died (Acts 18:24–28).

1. As Paul came to the city, he found some disciples who had apparently been taught by Apollos. Paul asked these men a very interesting question: "Did you receive the Holy Spirit when you believed?" They gave an equally interesting answer: "We have not even heard whether there is a Holy Spirit."

2. Paul then asked the most critical question in understanding how a person receives the Holy Spirit: "Into what then were you baptized?"

He clearly implies, by asking the question in this manner, that they should have received the Holy Spirit by being baptized into something. What was the something that they should have been baptized into?

Romans 6:3 and Galatians 3:27 make it clear that a person is baptized into Christ Jesus. There is no other way—anyone who tries to get into Christ another way is a thief and a robber (John 10:1).

In being immersed into Christ, a person is born again as he is buried with Christ in baptism, and rises to walk in newness of life (Romans 6:4). Baptism is not merely a symbol of these things, nor is it a public testimony of salvation which has already taken place—the plain teaching of the scripture is that *these things occur in immersion!*

These men of Ephesus should have received the Holy Spirit upon being immersed into Christ Jesus!

3. In answering Paul's question about what they were immersed into, the men replied: "Into John's baptism." Paul explained to them that John baptized with the baptism of repentance, telling the people to believe in Him who was coming later—Jesus.

   What was the baptism of repentance? According to Mark 1:4 and Luke 3:3, the baptism of repentance was for the forgiveness of sins, but that only took care of their past. They needed something more.

4. When Paul explained these things to the men, they were then immersed in the name of Jesus.

   We recall that Paul's concern in the matter was whether these men received the Holy Spirit. They had been baptized into John's baptism, which did not promise the Holy Spirit. When Paul explained everything to them, they were now baptized in Jesus' name, which did promise the Holy Spirit! Since they had received forgiveness of sins, it is clear that they were baptized this second time to receive the Holy Spirit. As Paul said, "If anyone does not have the Spirit of Christ, he does not belong to Him" (Romans 8:9).

5. Then Paul laid hands on them, and they spoke in tongues and prophesied. These are gifts of the Spirit, and we will deal with this more completely in the next section.

John 3:5

1. In John 3, a man named Nicodemus, who was one of the ranking Pharisees, came to Jesus by night. Jesus explained to him that unless one was "*born again*" he could not see the kingdom of God. Nicodemus wanted to know what Jesus meant by "*born again.*" Jesus explained that unless a person was born "of water and Spirit," he could not enter into the kingdom of God.

2. What is the kingdom of God? Without going into it too deeply at this point, the kingdom of God is the church. (See the study *Christ's Church*, the section dealing with the kingdom of God.) Colossians 1:13 makes it clear that Christians are already in the kingdom of Christ. A comparison of Matthew 16:28 and Mark 9:1 shows that the kingdom of God already exists, and it is the church.

3. Jesus points out that entrance into the kingdom of God is conditional: a person must be born of water *and* Spirit. We have already seen that entrance into Christ is obtained through immersion in water (Romans 6:3; Galatians 3:27). Entrance into Christ's body (which is the church—Ephesians 1:22,23), as one would expect, is obtained in that same immersion (I Corinthians 12:13).

4. Since entrance into the church is obtained through immersion in water, the entrance into the kingdom of God is also obtained in that same immersion. But Jesus makes it plain that one

21

cannot enter the kingdom without the Holy Spirit. Therefore, one must receive the Holy Spirit at the exact moment of his immersion in water in Jesus' name for the forgiveness of sins.

Note that this is consistent with the conclusion that we came to in examining Acts 19. And this makes the meaning of Acts 2:38 clear—a person is given the indwelling presence of the Holy Spirit upon being immersed in Jesus' name for the forgiveness of sins.

Summary

The Bible makes it clear, from a couple of different perspectives, that we receive the Holy Spirit at the point of our immersion into Christ Jesus. This is a key point, because there is no other way to receive the Holy Spirit, and without Him we do not belong to Christ. There is no example in the Bible of anyone receiving the Holy Spirit by "accepting Jesus into their hearts," or in any other way that men might devise. The Holy Spirit is given "to those who obey Him" (Acts 5:32) by believing the testimony of the Word of God, repenting, confessing the Lord Jesus with the mouth, and being immersed into Jesus.

Being born "of water and Spirit."

IV. THE GIFTS OF THE HOLY SPIRIT

Today many people claim the gifts of the Holy Spirit, including speaking in tongues. We have some questions for which we want Bible answers.

What Are the Gifts of the Holy Spirit?

In I Corinthians 12:4–11 Paul gives a list of the gifts, which includes faith, knowledge, ability to work miracles, etc. Paul does say that the gifts were distributed as the Holy Spirit willed, but nowhere in I Corinthians are we told how the gifts were given by the Holy Spirit.

How Were the Gifts Given in the Bible?

Because the Spirit is the same today, yesterday, and forever (Hebrews 13:8), and because the Holy Spirit never operates in a manner contradictory to His written word (John 10:35), the Holy Spirit gives the gifts in the same way now as He did in the New Testament.

Acts 8:14–19

A man named Philip (not Philip the apostle—the apostles stayed behind in Jerusalem—Acts 8:1), who was one of the seven men set apart for some special work in the Jerusalem church in Acts 6:1–6, went to Samaria to preach the gospel. As Philip preached, he confirmed the word with signs and wonders, and many Samaritans believed and were being immersed in the name of Jesus.

When the apostles in Jerusalem heard that Samaria had received the word of God, they sent Peter and John "Who came down and prayed for them, that they might receive the Holy Spirit. For He had not yet fallen upon any of them; they had simply been baptized in the name of the Lord Jesus. Then they began laying their hands on them and they were receiving the Holy Spirit" (Acts 8:15–17).

⋙ Consider these points: ⋘

1. The scripture does not contradict itself.
2. The baptism with the Holy Spirit is not indicated here, for the baptism with the Spirit was given by Jesus (not the apostles), and consisted of a sound like a mighty wind, tongues like fire, and speaking in other tongues.
3. The indwelling of the Spirit is not indicated here, for the indwelling was given at baptism in Jesus' name, and these people had all been immersed in the name of Christ.
4. Whatever it was concerning the Spirit that was given in Samaria, it was given through the laying on of the apostles' hands.

Let's guess that it was the gifts of the Spirit which were given in this fashion—and let's test our guess by digging further into the scripture.

I Corinthians 14:26–33

In I Corinthians 14 we find that two gifts in particular are mentioned—the gift of tongues and the gift of prophecy. Paul gives some specific instructions concerning these two gifts. If there was no interpreter, the use of the gift of tongues was to keep silent in the church. Similarly, the prophet was to stop speaking and let another talk, if that other received a revelation while the first was prophesying. The gift of prophecy was under the control of the user, as Paul said in verse 30: "The spirits of the prophets are subject to the prophets."

The principle evident in the use of the spiritual gifts is that the user of the gift is in control of his own gift and can use it—or not use it—or misuse it—at his own discretion.

II Timothy 1:6

Paul, an apostle of Jesus Christ, tells Timothy to "rekindle the gift of God that is in you by the laying on of my hands." A gift that one is to rekindle or "fire up" is a gift which is under the control of the user. Notice the parallel between the gift that was in Timothy and the gifts of I Corinthians 14—in both cases the user was the one who controlled his gifts.

Furthermore, notice that Timothy's gift was in him by the laying on of an apostle's hands.

Stephen and Philip

In Acts 6:6 the apostles laid hands on seven men. In Acts 6:8, we find Stephen, one of those seven, suddenly performing great signs and miracles—after the apostles laid hands on him.

In Acts 8:4–7 we find Philip, another of the seven men of Acts 6:6, performing signs and miracles—again after the apostles laid hands on him.

Acts 19:6

In Acts 19, Paul immersed about 12 men in the name of Jesus for the forgiveness of sins and that they might receive the gift of the Holy Spirit. In verse 6, Paul laid hands on them; then they began to speak in tongues and prophesy.

The gifts of the Spirit, without exception, are given in the New Testament by the laying on of the apostles' hands. Since the Holy Spirit continues to operate in the same way now as He did in the New Testament, and since there are no apostles of Jesus Christ now, no one in our time can receive the gifts of the Holy Spirit.

What Was the Duration of the Gifts?

A cross–check on our conclusion in the above section is found in I Corinthians 13:8–13. After exhorting the Corinthians to use their gifts in love, Paul then compares something that is "in part" with something that is "perfect." He points out that the gifts of prophecy, knowledge, and tongues are temporary—they are in part. Then he compares them to something that is perfect.

The words translated "the perfect" are the Greek words to *telion*—a something, not a someone. The scripture here refers to something that is complete, in contrast to something that is partial.

The only thing which is "complete" which can be contrasted with the "partial" is the New Testament. The New Testament is now complete, but was only in the making at the time that Paul was writing his Holy Spirit–inspired letters to churches such as at Corinth. The gifts were "partial" and were only in use until the "complete" came. With the coming of the New Testament, the gifts were phased out.

Even Paul only "knew in part and prophesied in part." But when the New Testament was completed, these "childish things" were done away, and now the mature church in the "man" stage could begin to operate. Men then could see themselves incompletely, but with the coming of the complete "word of God" which is able to "judge the thoughts and intentions of the heart" (Hebrews 4:12), now we can know ourselves "fully" just as we have been "fully known." So it is possible for a person who studies and understands the Bible today to have a better comprehension of the things of God than the apostle Paul had!

Once again, this checks with the conclusion which we reached from a different direction—that the gifts of the Spirit died out when the apostles died, and could no longer pass them on by the laying on of their hands. The New Testament was completed when John the apostle wrote his last letters and the book of Revelation sometime near 100 A.D. Most of the other apostles had been dead for 30 or 40 years by this time.

Gifts of the Spirit

—were given by the apostles
—were under the control of the user
—were in use until the New Testament was complete
—disappeared as the apostles died
—were given to establish a church

What Was the Purpose of the Gifts?

In the New Testament church, before the New Testament was completed, it would be very important for someone to have the various gifts of the Spirit. To know that Jesus is going to return soon, we have the book of Revelation—they needed someone with the gift of prophecy. To know the qualifications of elders, we have the text of I Timothy—they had someone with the gift of knowledge. To know that Jesus was raised from the dead in accordance with the Old Testament scriptures, we have the great messages of the book of Acts—they needed to confirm the word with "signs and miracles and by gifts of the Holy Spirit" (Hebrews 2:3,4).

Today we can say the Bible says such and such and quote the scripture, but how could they "test the spirits?" It would be important that someone in the congregation have the gift of "distinguishing of spirits" to see whether the individual who said "Thus says the Lord!" was telling the truth.

That's why it was necessary for Peter and John, apostles of Jesus Christ, to come up to Samaria from Jerusalem and lay hands on the Samaritans. Philip was about to leave Samaria and there would be no one who could teach them further about the kingdom of God. So these two apostles came up and laid hands on them, and the Holy Spirit gave the gifts as He willed, and the church in Samaria was established (see Romans 1:11), "not lacking any gift" (I Corinthians 1:7).

26

Summary

The gifts of the Holy Spirit were given by the laying on of the apostles' hands. They consisted of about ten different specialties and were necessary in the early church, lasting until the writings of the New Testament were completed. The user of the spiritual gift was in control at all times, and was exhorted to use his gift in a spirit of love.

V. THE FILLING WITH THE HOLY SPIRIT

Before Christ's Death

The filling with the Holy Spirit occurred in Old Testament times and under the Old Covenant before Jesus died on the cross (see Hebrews 9:16,17). In Luke 1:67, John the Baptist's father was filled with the Holy Spirit and prophesied. Peter pointed out that such men spoke when they were "moved by the Holy Spirit" (II Peter 1:21).

Such filling with the Spirit was beyond the control of the one so filled, and the individual did not even understand the significance of what he said most of the time. These men of old wanted to know from God "what person or time the Spirit of Christ within them was indicating" (I Peter 1:11), but "it was revealed to them that they were not serving themselves" (I Peter 1:12).

The filling with the Holy Spirit under the Old Testament dispensation is quite distinct from the New Testament command to "be filled with the Spirit" (Ephesians 5:18). New Testament "filling" requires conscious mental effort (see study entitled *The New Creation*) on the part of the Christian— Old Testament "filling" was quite beyond the control of the one so filled.

Special Filling with the Spirit in the Early Stages of the Church

In Acts 4:8 Peter was filled with the Holy Spirit while on trial before the Jewish High Council, the Sanhedrin. This was in accordance with the promise Jesus had given the apostles (and only the apostles—Mark 13:11).

In Acts 4:31 the disciples were filled with the Holy Spirit. This was apparently a sign from heaven at a critical time in the church's development—when they were under persecution for the first time. So God shook the place where they were gathered and gave them the ability to speak the word of God with boldness. Such a special sign was never again evidenced even in the early church.

Summary

Old Testament "filling," as contrasted with normal New Testament "filling with the Holy Spirit," was entirely beyond the control of the individual filled. God did fill the apostles with the Spirit when they were on trial, and He did manifest a special filling once when the church faced its first persecution.

VI. SUMMARY OF LESSON

The purpose of this study was to understand the operations of the Holy Spirit as explicitly spelled out in God's Word. The chart on the following page provides the summary of definitions and concepts that we have worked out concerning the operations of the Holy Spirit since Christ's death on the cross.

THE OPERATIONS OF THE HOLY SPIRIT UNDER THE NEW COVENANT

Baptism with Spirit	Indwelling Presence of Spirit	Gifts of the Spirit	Special Filling
Occurred only twice: 1. On the apostles to begin the church. 2. On Cornelius' household to extend salvation to the Gentiles.	**FOR EVERY CHRISTIAN** for all time, to make him "born again."	For Christians in the early church, to enable them to function without the Bible.	1. For apostles under trial. 2. A special sign when the church faced its first persecution.
Consisted of: 1. Sound like a mighty rushing wind. 2. Tongues like fire on the heads of those baptized. 3. Speaking in other tongues.	Consists of: The Holy Spirit coming to live inside the Christian and working within to make him like Christ.	Consisted of: About ten different specialities, such as prophecy, wisdom, and distinguishing of spirits.	Consisted of: 1. The apostles knowing what to say when on trial. 2. The building being shaken, and Christians speaking the word of God with boldness.
Given by Jesus as a powerful sign for the benefit of those of Jewish background who watched the sign occur.	Given by God when an individual is baptized by immersion in water for the forgiveness of sins, provided he believes, is repentant, and has confessed Christ as Lord.	Given by the Holy Spirit when the apostles laid hands on a Christian.	Given by God to keep the early church functioning at critical times.

SPECIAL STUDY—ACTS 2:16-18

Introduction

On the Day of Pentecost, the apostle Peter stood with the eleven and proclaimed for the first time the gospel of salvation. Responding to the charges that the apostles were drunk, he answered that they were baptized with the Holy Spirit by quoting from the prophet Joel: "But this is what was spoken of through the prophet Joel: 'And it shall be in the last days,' God says, 'That I will pour out My Spirit upon all flesh; and your sons and daughters shall prophesy and your young men shall see visions, and your old men shall dream dreams; even upon My bondslaves, both men and women, I will in those days pour forth of My Spirit, and they shall prophesy.'"

It is claimed by many today that "we are now in the last days. In these last days God's Spirit is working in all denominations to bring them together before He comes again. He is pouring forth of His Spirit—Christians of all denominations are having visions, and prophesying as He is showing us by these things that we are now in the last days."

We will see that such claims are no more than unadulterated hogwash.

Quick Review

In earlier sections we have seen that the baptism with the Holy Spirit occurred only twice for special purposes—to start the church and to spread salvation to the Gentiles. It came with three manifestations:

(1) A sound like a mighty rushing wind

(2) Tongues like fire

(3) Speaking in other languages.

All three manifestations must be present in order for a person to be baptized with the Holy Spirit—and no one today has been.

We have also seen that the various gifts of the Spirit were given by the laying on of the apostles' hands and therefore (since there are now no apostles), no one today has any such gift as prophecy or speaking in tongues.

So any claims to the contrary are spurious at best; outright lies at worst. So what is the meaning of Acts 2:16-18?

30

The Last Days

Peter is quoting from a prophecy some 800 years old as he justifies, by this prophecy, that the sign which had just fallen upon the apostles was in accordance with Old Testament scripture. Joel had said, "And it shall be in *the last days.*"

What were the "last days" from Joel's point of view? The writer of Hebrews explains: "God, after He spoke long ago to the fathers in the prophets in many portions and in many ways, in *these last days* has spoken to us in His Son …" (Hebrews 1:1,2).

In "the last days" God would "pour forth of My Spirit on all flesh." God first poured forth His Spirit upon the apostles—Jews. Then 10-13 years later He poured forth His Spirit upon the household of Cornelius—Gentiles (Acts 10 & 11). Thus His Spirit was poured forth upon "all flesh" in the baptism with the Spirit.

He also spoke of men and women, young and old, seeing visions, etc. This occurred in the early stages of the church as men and women were given gifts of the Spirit through the laying on of the apostles' hands.

In these two ways this portion of Joel's prophecy was thus fulfilled. (For the study on the last part of this prophecy quoted by Peter—Acts 2:19-21—see the study on *Christ's Church.*)

Conclusion

We have been in the last days since Christ died on the cross. Since Joel's prophecy was fulfilled in the early stages of the church, and since the means for receiving miraculous measures of the Spirit have now passed away, no one today exhibits the things Joel prophesied.

The Holy Spirit today works through His word. We have Moses and the prophets and the apostles. Hear them!

SPECIAL STUDY—THE BAPTISM WITH FIRE

As crowds flocked to hear John the Immerser, and to be immersed with the immersion of repentance for the forgiveness of sins (Luke 3:3), he told them, "As for me, I baptize you in water for repentance, but He who is coming after me is mightier than I, and I am not even fit to remove His sandals; He Himself will baptize you with the Holy Spirit and fire" (Matthew 3:11).

We have already seen how the apostles and the household of Cornelius were baptized with the Holy Spirit. But who was to be baptized with fire? The apostles? Cornelius? There were tongues like fire which came as a part of the baptism with the Spirit, but since they were part of the Spirit baptism, and since that is not an overwhelming immersion in fire, we are forced to conclude that the baptism with fire is something separate from the baptism with the Spirit.

John continues to give information about the coming One: "And His winnowing fork is in His hand, and He will thoroughly clean His threshing floor; and He will gather His wheat in the barn, but He will burn up the chaff with unquenchable *FIRE*" (Matthew 3:12).

The same One who opened the door of salvation to both Jew and Gentile by pouring forth the baptism with the Spirit—the One who opens and no one can shut—will also pour forth the baptism with fire on those who reject His word in the day of the wrath of the Lamb of God. Jesus has been given authority to execute judgment (John 5:27), and He will burn the chaff on that Day with the baptism with fire.

THE HOLY SPIRIT

Instructions: *This set of questions is divided into two sections—Specific Questions and General Questions. The Specific Questions bring out many details in the study, and help you to understand many of the important points, and where in the scripture to find answers to many common questions. The General Questions help you pick out the major ideas and concepts in the study. You may use your Bible and the study booklet for the Specific Questions, but try to answer the General Questions from memory.*

Each section is divided into subsections, each of which has its own type of questions and its attendant instructions.

<u>Specific Questions</u>

True or False?

_____ 1. Jesus promised to send the Holy Spirit after He returned to heaven.

_____ 2. The most important question in the Bible is: "Did you receive the Holy Spirit when you believed?"

_____ 3. Confidence in our salvation must be based on our inner feelings toward God—if we feel confident of our salvation, then we know we have the Holy Spirit.

_____ 4. The Holy Spirit came to glorify Himself.

_____ 5. Teachings about the Holy Spirit are scattered throughout the New Testament.

Answer the following questions.

1. What did God mean in Genesis 1:26 when He said, "Let Us make man in Our image"? _____

33

_____

_____

_____

_____

2. Explain the meaning of "immersed into the name of the Father and the Son and the Holy Spirit" of Matthew 28:19,20. _____

_____

_____

3. Discuss John 14:28; Hebrews 5:8, in relationship to Hebrews 1:8 and Isaiah 9:6 in regard to the person of Jesus. _____

_____

_____

_____

_____

_____

_____

4. Comment on John 14:16,17, and Colossians 2:9 concerning the relationship of Jesus to the Holy Spirit. _____

_____

_____

_____

_____

5. Why was it to the apostles' advantage that Jesus go away in John 16:7? Explain in some detail. _____

_____

_____

_____

_____

_____

6. List four names for the Holy Spirit found in Romans 8:9-11.

   a) _____

   b) _____

   c) _____

   d) _____

7. Who is the Holy Spirit? _____

_____

_____

_____

_____

_____

True or False?

_____   1. The Bible has many references to the baptism of the Holy Ghost.

_____   2. A key questions is: What is God's definition of the baptism with the Holy Spirit?

_____   3. John the Immerser promised that Jesus would baptize with the Holy Spirit.

_____ 4. John promised that every Christian would be baptized with the Holy Spirit.

_____ 5. Jesus had hundreds of apostles, but only 12 disciples.

_____ 6. Jesus appeared to the apostles a number of times over a period of 40 days.

_____ 7. Jesus promised 120 disciples that they would be baptized with the Holy Spirit within several days.

Multiple Choice. More than one answer may be correct; show all correct answers.

_____ 1. The baptism with the Holy Spirit consists of:
   a) Sound like a mighty wind
   b) Laying on of hands
   c) Tongues like fire
   d) Speaking in other languages

_____ 2. The Day of Pentecost:
   a) Is the day the church began
   b) Was the Jewish feast day originally called the "feast of weeks"
   c) Came 50 days after Passover
   d) Continues to occur every week

_____ 3. All male Jews were required:
   a) To be in Jerusalem on three major Jewish feast days
   b) To shave their heads
   c) To present themselves to the Lord at the temple
   d) To be scattered throughout Pontus and Asia

_____ 4. The baptism with the Holy Spirit:
   a) Occurs nearly every day someplace in the world
   b) Was promised by Jesus to the apostles ten days prior to Pentecost
   c) Happened only to the apostles
   d) In the New Testament happened many times

_____5. The apostles:
   a) Consisted of 120 people
   b) Were all Galileans
   c) Were the ones who spoke in tongues on the day of Pentecost
   d) Were in one place in the temple

_____6. Cornelius:
   a) Was Gentile
   b) Had a vision in which an angel appeared to him
   c) Was the first Gentile to be saved
   d) Rejected the Lord

_____7. Peter:
   a) Had a vision from the Lord
   b) Had a hard time understanding that the Gentiles were acceptable to God
   c) Preached the gospel to Cornelius and his friends and family
   d) Ordered Cornelius and his household to be immersed

_____8. When Peter arrived:
   a) Cornelius met them and fell down to worship at Peter's feet
   b) Peter told Cornelius not to worship him
   c) Peter apologized for being there
   d) Peter had Cornelius kiss his ring

_____9. At the household of Cornelius:
   a) Peter preached the message of the death, burial, and resurrection of the Messiah
   b) The Holy Spirit fell upon the Gentiles who were there
   c) Peter and those who were with him were baptized with the Holy Spirit
   d) Everyone had a big party

_____10. In Acts chapter 11:
   a) Peter's story contradicts that of Acts chapter 10

b) The Jewish Christians in Jerusalem challenged Peter's going to the Gentiles

c) A meeting is described in which Peter is portraying what happened in Acts 10

d) Peter had six brethren with him as witnesses

_____11. Acts 11:15:

a) Is the key verse in Acts 11 in understanding the baptism with the Spirit

b) Compares what had happened to Cornelius with what had happened at the beginning

c) Makes it clear that what happened to Cornelius happened to the apostles at the beginning

d) Makes it clear that the Holy Spirit fell on the apostles on the day of Pentecost

_____12. In Acts 11:16:

a) Peter is confused

b) Peter quotes Acts 15

c) Peter excoriates the Jewish Christians

d) Defines what was described in Acts 11:15 as the baptism with the Spirit

True or False?

_____ 1. Prior to the conversion of Cornelius some Gentiles were saved.

_____ 2. In Acts 10 God prepared Peter for the salvation of the Gentiles.

_____ 3. The angel told Cornelius that he and his household would hear words by which they would be saved.

_____ 4. Peter had a vision of a great sheet being let down with unclean animals on it and was told to "rise, kill and eat."

_____ 5. The Holy Spirit sent some men to bring Peter with them.

_____ 6. Peter did not think it strange to go to the house of a Gentile.

_____ 7. Peter preached a message to Cornelius and his family and friends proving that Jesus was resurrected from the dead and was the Messiah.

_____ 8. While Peter was still speaking the Holy Spirit fell upon the Gentiles who were there.

_____ 9. It is not clear from Acts 10 exactly what happened to the Gentiles in regard to the Holy Spirit.

_____ 10. Peter's reaction to all of this was that all of those who had received the outpouring of the Holy Spirit were to be immersed in water in the name of Jesus Christ.

_____ 11. Acts 11 makes clear what happened in Acts 10.

_____ 12. When Peter got back to Jerusalem he had to explain to the Jewish Christians there why he had gone to the house of Gentiles and eaten with them.

_____ 13. In Acts 11:15 Peter said that the Holy Spirit fell upon them "just as upon us at the beginning."

_____ 14. The "beginning " is the Day of Pentecost.

_____ 15. The "us" at the beginning were the apostles.

_____ 16. The word "just" means "exactly the same way as."

_____ 17. It is clear from Acts 11 that the baptism with the Holy Spirit consists of three things: 1) a sound like a mighty wind, 2) tongues like fire coming down from heaven, and 3) speaking in other languages as the Spirit gave utterance.

_____ 18. In Acts 11:16 Peter makes it clear that what had happened in Acts 10 was the baptism of the Spirit.

_____ 19. The "we" of Acts 10:47 is the 120 disciples of Acts 1:15.

_____ 20. The result of the household of Cornelius being baptized with the Holy Spirit was that they were saved at this point.

39

_____ 21. The Gentiles with Cornelius had to be immersed in water to be saved.

_____ 22. Peter describes the turning of the Gentiles to Christ as the repentance that led to life—Acts 11:18.

_____ 23. In Acts 2:33 Peter defines the baptism with the Spirit as something which is both visible and audible.

_____ 24. Peter and the Jews with him were amazed when the Holy Spirit was poured out on the Gentiles.

_____ 25. The day of Pentecost came 10 days after Jesus' ascension.

Fill in the Blanks.

1. On the day of Pentecost recorded in _____ _____ Peter preached the first gospel sermon. As a result of hearing the message proclaimed that day _____ were immersed in the name of Jesus _____ _____ _____ _____ _____ _____ _____.

2. On the Day of Pentecost the purpose of the baptism with the Spirit was to _____ _____ _____ _____ _____ _____.

3. Cornelius' household was also _____ _____ _____ _____ _____ as a sign to those of _____ background.

4. The baptism with the Spirit provided _____ to _____ Christians in other locations that Gentiles were _____ _____ _____.

5. Because of Jewish prejudice against Gentiles the _____ was to remove Peter's unwillingness to have the Gentiles _____ _____ _____.

6. In Cornelius' case the baptism _____ _____ _____ was not for the benefit _____ _____ _____ at all. It was strictly a sign for the benefit of

_____ _____ that the Gentiles could now

_____ ____ _____.

7. Jesus had promised Peter, "I will give you the _____ ____

_____ _____ ____ _____; and whatever

you bind on earth shall _____ _____ _____ ____

_____. And whatever you loose on earth shall

have been _____ ____ _____ "

(Matthew 16:19).

8. On the Day of Pentecost _____ used the keys to the

kingdom to open the door of salvation to the _____ and

the _____ after the baptism of the Spirit had been

given from _____.

9. Peter used the _____ to open the door of salvation to

the _____ after the sign that _____ ____

_____ _____ _____ had been given

from heaven.

10. The only purpose of the baptism with the Spirit was to be _____

_____ ____ _____, first to begin the church, then to open

salvation to the Gentiles. In both cases the _____

was for the benefit of the _____ watching and not for

the benefit of those _____ ____ _____ _____.

11. There was no evidence that _____ and his household

had any power at all following their being _____

_____ _____ _____.

12. It was necessary for Cornelius and his household to be

_____ in water in Jesus' name _____ _____

_____ ___ _____.

13. There is no evidence that _____ was ever baptized

with the Spirit but he had all the power of _____

_____ ___ _____ _____.

14. There are only 2 occasions where anyone was

_____ with the Holy Spirit.

41

Matching.

_____ 1. II Timothy 1:14

_____ 2. Acts 2:38

_____ 3. John's immersion

_____ 4. "Did you receive the Holy Spirit when you believed?"

_____ 5. "Into what then were you immersed?"

_____ 6. Acts 19:5

a) Romans 6:3; Galatians 3:27.

b) Immersed into the name of Christ.

c) Immersion of repentance for the forgiveness of sins

d) "We have not even heard whether there is a Holy Spirit."

e) The Spirit dwells in Christians.

f) Something connected with the Spirit is received at a person's immersion into Christ.

True or False?

_____ 1. Nicodemus wanted to know how to be born again. Jesus explained to him that a person is born again of Spirit only.

_____ 2. The kingdom of God is the Church.

_____ 3. A person enters the kingdom of God when he is born of water and Spirit.

_____ 4. A person is immersed into the body of Christ.

_____ 5. Being born again of water and Spirit occurs at a person's immersion into Christ.

_____ 6. A person can enter the church without the Holy Spirit.

_____ 7. John 3:3-5 coupled with I Corinthians 12:13 makes it clear that a person receives the Spirit at his immersion into Christ.

Answer the following questions:

1. Explain how Acts 19:1-5 shows that a person must receive the indwelling presence of the Spirit at his immersion into Christ. __

_____

_____

_____

_____

2. Show how John 3:5 makes it clear that a person must receive the Spirit at his immersion into Christ _____

_____

_____

_____

_____

3. List the gifts of the Holy Spirit. _____

_____

_____

_____

_____

4. Explain the apparent contradiction of Acts 2:38 and Acts 8:15-17.

_____

_____

_____

_____

5. Show how I Corinthians 14:26-33 and II Timothy 1:6 are connected. _____

_____

_____

_____

_____

_____

6. Explain the relationship between the laying on of hands on Stephen and Philip, Acts 19:6, and the gifts of the Spirit. _____

_____

_____

_____

_____

7. Explain the relationship of the "partial" to the "perfect" in I Corinthians 13:8-10. _____

_____

_____

_____

_____

8. Compare the church to a child and the church to a man and relate it to I Corinthians 13:11. _____

_____

_____

_____

_____

9. Explain what it means to be "fully known...." _____

_____

_____

_____

_____

_____

10. Describe the importance of the gifts for the church in New Testament times. _____

_____

_____

_____

_____

_____

True or False?

_____ 1. There are apostles of Jesus Christ today.

_____ 2. The baptism with the Spirit is given through the laying on of hands of the apostles.

_____ 3. A person receives the indwelling presence of the Spirit by asking Jesus into his heart.

_____ 4. The gifts of the Spirit were for New Testament times only.

_____ 5. The only way a person can receive a gift of the Spirit is through the laying on of hands of one of the apostles of Jesus Christ.

_____ 6. Because the word of God is not complete today, we still need spiritual gifts to operate in our churches.

_____ 7. In Acts 8 it was necessary for Peter and John to come up from Jerusalem to lay hands on the people of Samaria so that they might receive the gifts of the Spirit.

_____ 8. The expression "gift of the Holy Spirit" sometimes refers to the indwelling presence of the Spirit and sometimes refers to the baptism with the Spirit. The context dictates the meaning.

_____ 9. If a person does not have the Spirit of Christ he does not belong to Jesus.

_____ 10. The purpose of the gifts of the Holy Spirit was to enable the church to function in the absence of the completed word.

_____ 11. Without exception no one received the gifts of the Holy Spirit in the New Testament without the laying on of the hands of the apostles.

_____ 12. The baptism with the Holy Spirit only occurred twice, once to begin the church and once to extend salvation to the Gentiles.

_____ 13. Nicodemus couldn't be born again when Jesus told him how because the kingdom of God had not yet come.

_____ 14. In Acts 19, twelve men were immersed into Christ to receive the indwelling presence of the Spirit. Then Paul laid hands on them so they might receive the gifts of tongues and prophecy.

_____ 15. Timothy had one of the gifts of the Spirit in him through the laying on of the apostle Paul's hands.

_____ 16. There are prophets and miracle workers today.

_____ 17. There are no contradictions in the word of God.

_____ 18. It is important that we let God define His own terms.

_____ 19. The indwelling presence of the Spirit is what is of primary importance.

_____ 20. It is possible for people today to be indwelled by the Holy Spirit of God.

Multiple Choice. More than one answer may be correct; show all correct answers.

_____1. The filling with the Holy Spirit in the Old Testament:
   a) Never occurred.
   b) Was uncontrolled by Old Testament prophets.
   c) Occurred in such men as David and Elijah
   d) Happened to Zacharias, father of John the Immerser.

_____2. Old Testament prophets:
   a) Did not understand most of what they said about the New Covenant.
   b) Were usually speaking for the benefit of the nation of Israel.
   c) Were unconcerned about knowledge of Christ.
   d) Looked forward to the period of the grace of God.

_____3. New Testament filling:
   a) Is different from Old Testament filling.
   b) Occurred in special cases in the New Testament.
   c) Never occurred.
   d) Occurs today in a different sense than special filling in the New Testament.

_____4. The apostles:
   a) Were all crucified as recorded in the pages of the New Testament.
   b) Were promised special information from the Spirit while on trial.
   c) Went their way and never saw each other again.
   d) Were sometimes specially filled with the Spirit.

_____5. The early church:
   a) Experienced the special filling of the Spirit at a critical time in church history.
   b) Experienced the special filling of the Spirit on a number of occasions.
   c) Operated in accordance with strict instructions in the Old Testament.
   d) Continued to operate under the terms of the ten commandments.

Answer the following questions:

1. Acts 2:16-18 is quoted from what Old Testament scripture? ____

   _____

   _____

2. Explain what the term "the last days" means. _____

   _____

   _____

   _____

   _____

   _____

3. Explain why Peter quoted Joel 2 in Acts 2. _____

   _____

   _____

   _____

   _____

4. Explain the meaning of "Pour forth my Spirit upon all flesh." __

   _____

   _____

   _____

   _____

5. Explain the meaning of men and women, young and old, seeing visions. _____

_____

_____

_____

_____

6. Describe the baptism with fire in relationship to the baptism with the Holy Spirit ._____

_____

_____

_____

_____

General Questions

1. List the five major sections of this study:

   a) _____

   b) _____

   c) _____

   d) _____

   e) _____

2. Who is the Holy Spirit? _____

   _____

   _____

   How do you find out about Him? _____

   _____

   How does He work? _____

   _____

49

3. John the Immerser promised that Jesus would baptize "you" with the Holy Spirit. Is "you" defined by John, or did he leave the word undefined? _____

4. On the day that Jesus ascended into heaven, He promised the _____ that they would be baptized with the Holy Spirit within a few days.

5. The first occurrence of the baptism with the Holy Spirit took place the Jewish feast day of _____, which was _____ days after Jesus' resurrection and _____ days after His ascension.

6. Three things happened to the apostles in the Temple on the day of Pentecost. List them:

   a) _____

   b) _____

   c) _____

   These three things constitute the _____

   _____.

7. As a result of the baptism with the Spirit, the _____ came together. Peter preached the first _____, and _____ Jews were immersed by the authority of Jesus for the forgiveness of their sins. This was the beginning of the _____.

8. For about 10 years after the beginning of the church, only_____ and _____ heard and obeyed the message of _____.

9. Peter and six brethren were sent to the house of a Gentile soldier named _____. As Peter preached to this man and those whom he had assembled, the _____ _____ was poured out upon the Gentiles.

10. As a result of this outpouring, Peter answered, "Surely no one can refuse _____ for these to be immersed who have received the Holy Spirit just as _____ did, can he?" And he ordered them to be immersed _____ _____ _____ _____ _____ _____.

_____ (give book, chapter, and verses).

12. Acts 11:15 reads: _____

_____

_____

The "beginning" is _____ _____ _____ _____, when the church began. The "us" at the beginning refers to _____ _____. The word "just" in this context means _____ _____

_____.

13. In reading Acts 11:15, we know that three things happened to Cornelius and his household. List them:

a) _____

b) _____

c) _____

14. In Acts 11:16, Peter describes the occurrence recorded in Acts 10 & 11 as the _____ _____ _____ _____ _____.

15. The baptism with the Spirit was sent the first time to _____ _____ _____. It was sent the second time to open salvation to the _____. In both cases it was a sign for the _____.

16. The baptism with the Holy Spirit was not a _____ for, and did not set aside the necessity of _____ _____ _____ _____.

_____ 1. According to Romans 8:9-11, the Holy Spirit dwells within Christians.

_____ 2. An important question is: "When does the Spirit enter the believer?"

_____ 3. Acts 2:38 contains enough information to make it clear that an individual receives the indwelling gift of the Spirit at his repentance and immersion in Christ's name for the forgiveness of his sins.

_____ 4. Paul asked 12 men in Ephesus if they had received the Holy Spirit when they believed.

_____ 5. These 12 men in Ephesus should have been immersed into Christ, but had only been immersed into John's immersion.

_____ 6. The difference between immersion in Christ's name and John's immersion is that the Holy Spirit was not received in John's immersion, and He is received in immersion in Christ's name.

_____ 7. The Scriptures make it clear that Paul accepted the previous immersion of the twelve disciples in Ephesus, and extended to them the right hand of fellowship.

_____ 8. A person can be a part of the kingdom of God without being born of the Spirit.

_____ 9. A person enters the body of Christ (the kingdom of God) when he is immersed in water for the remission of his sins.

_____ 10. An individual must receive the Holy Spirit at his immersion to be born of water and Spirit.

Multiple Choice. More than one answer may be correct; show all correct answers.

_____ 1. The gifts of the Holy Spirit include:

a) Tongues like fire.

b) Discerning of spirits.

c) Speaking in tongues.

d) Sound like a mighty wind.

_____ 2.   In Acts 8:12-19:

a)   The Holy Spirit was given through the laying on of the apostle Philip's hands.

b)   The people were immersed in Jesus' name, but never received the indwelling Holy Spirit.

c)   There is a contradiction of scripture.

d)   The gifts of the Spirit were given through the laying on of the hands of the apostles Peter and John.

_____ 3.   In I Corinthians 14:26-33:

a)   All things were to be done for edification.

b)   Once the Spirit took control of the individual he went into a trance, and did whatever the Spirit impelled him to do.

c)   The spirits of the prophets were subject to the prophets.

d)   The gifts could be used, abused, misused.

_____ 4.   In II Timothy 1:6:

a)   The apostle Paul wrote to Timothy.

b)   Timothy was told to rekindle his gift.

c)   Timothy's gift was in him through the laying on of Paul's hands.

d)   Timothy was exhorted to be baptized with the '] Spirit.

_____ 5.   In the book of Acts:

a)   Paul was baptized with the Holy Spirit.

b)   Stephen received the gifts of the Spirit after the apostles laid hands on him.

c)   Philip received the gifts after the apostles laid hands on him.

d)   Twelve men in Ephesus spoke in foreign languages and prophesied after Paul laid hands on them.

_____ 6. The gifts of the Holy Spirit:

    a) Lasted until the completion of the New Testament.

    b) Are for those who have enough faith to ask for them.

    c) Can be passed on by one of the modern apostles.

    d) Were important to the functioning of the local churches in the absence of the written New Testament.

_____ 7. Old Covenant filling with the Spirit:

    a) Was beyond the control of the one so filled.

    b) Was just like New Covenant filling.

    c) Was the means by which Old Testament prophets spoke.

    d) Occurred only twice.

_____ 8. Special filling with the Spirit under the New Covenant:

    a) Occurred only twice.

    b) Was promised to the apostles while on trial.

    c) Is recorded throughout the book of Acts.

    d) Occurred at a very early stage in the church's history, when its existence was seriously threatened by the forces of evil.

Made in the USA
Columbia, SC
13 January 2025

51724536R00037